MEETING
BOB
PROCTOR
SECOND EDITION

A MEMOIR
OF
A GREAT MAN

MEETING
BOB
PROCTOR
SECOND EDITION

A MEMOIR
OF
A GREAT MAN

ADRIAN MAXWELL

DEDICATION

To the memory of Bob Proctor

Table of Contents

FOREWORD

A Personal Tribute to Bob Proctor: The Man Who Changed Everything

Hello, my name is Adrian, and as I write these words, my heart is still heavy with the profound emotion that swept over me when I learned of Bob Proctor's passing. At 87 years of age, this giant of personal development, this beacon of hope for millions, this extraordinary life success coach and mentor, left our physical world on February 3, 2022. Yet even as I mourn his departure, I find myself overwhelmed with gratitude for the immeasurable gift he was to humanity, and to me personally.

Bob Proctor didn't just change lives; he revolutionized them. He took broken spirits and showed them how to soar. He took poverty consciousness and transformed it into prosperity thinking. He took my own life, shattered and directionless in the darkness of rock bottom in the 1990s, and illuminated a path toward a future I never dared imagine possible. This is why I feel compelled, no, called, to share this tribute to a man whose wisdom transcended mere motivational speaking and touched the very essence of human potential.

When Bob passed, I felt as though a very wise and important light had been extinguished from this world. It was as if a library of ancient wisdom, a fountain of endless encouragement, and a torch that had guided so many through their darkest nights had suddenly gone dim. But here's what I've come to understand: while Bob Proctor the man may have left us, the gift of his wisdom, the power of his teachings, and the ripple effects of his influence continue to expand across the universe like waves that never cease.

Bob was an amazing influence on my life, that's an understatement that hardly does justice to the transformation he sparked within me. And I know, with absolute certainty, that he's been that same catalytic force in the lives of countless others around the globe. From boardrooms to living rooms, from those struggling with bankruptcy to those seeking to break through to their next level of success, Bob's teachings have been the bridge between where people were and where they dreamed to be.

I don't even know where to begin really to explain the magnitude of his impact. How do you capture in words the moment when someone's teaching suddenly makes everything click? How do you describe the feeling when decades of limiting beliefs crumble in an instant, replaced by an unshakeable knowing that you are capable of so much more? But I'll try, because I believe Bob would want me to. He'd want all of us who've been touched by his work to carry the torch forward.

I understand the skeptics. Sometimes people look at the vast world of self-help and personal development and think, "There's all this material out there, all these promises, but does it really help?" They wonder with genuine uncertainty, "Does it really work? Is this just feel-good philosophy, or can it create tangible, lasting change?" They think to themselves, "I hear it's worked for one person, maybe someone who was already privileged or lucky, but can it really work for me? Can it work for someone who's truly at rock bottom, someone who's tried everything else?"

I think there's a lot of doubt in the world still, and perhaps there always will be. We live in an age of information overload, where everyone claims to have the secret to success, the key to happiness, the formula for wealth. It's natural to be skeptical. It's even healthy to question. Bob himself would tell you to test everything, to prove it to yourself through application, not just accept it on faith.

I know there are people out there right now, perhaps you who are reading this, who are doubting whether the teachings of someone like Bob Proctor could really change their life. Maybe you've tried before and failed. Maybe you've read the books, attended the seminars, repeated the affirmations, and still find yourself stuck in the same patterns, the same circumstances, the same limitations. Maybe you're wondering if you're somehow different, somehow unable to access the transformation that others claim to have found.

But let me tell you a little bit about my story, not because my story is unique, but precisely because it isn't. Because if someone like me, starting from where I started, facing what I faced, could experience the transformation I experienced through Bob's teachings, then I believe with every fiber of my being that you can too. Perhaps as you read about my journey from desperation to inspiration, from scarcity to abundance, from merely existing to truly living, you will start to see just how powerful a great teacher and mentor can be in someone's life.

Bob Proctor often said, "Most people are extras in their own movie." Well, he taught me how to become the director, the producer, and the star of mine. He showed me that the script I'd been following was one I'd unconsciously accepted, not one I'd consciously chosen. And most importantly, he gave me the tools to rewrite that script entirely.

What follows is not just my story, but a testament to the enduring legacy of a man who dedicated his life to awakening others to their infinite potential. It's a celebration of Bob Proctor's teachings, distilled through the lens of one life he touched among millions. And it's an invitation, to you, dear reader, to consider that perhaps, just perhaps, the doubt you feel is simply the last barrier between you and the life you've always imagined.

Bob may have left this physical plane, but his voice still echoes in the principles he taught, in the lives he changed, and in the potential that lies dormant within you, waiting to be awakened. This is my tribute to him, and my gift to you, proof that transformation isn't just possible; it's your birthright.

Welcome to the journey. Bob would be thrilled to know you're here.

Adrian

LOSING AND FINDING THE LEGENDARY BOB PROCTOR

The Day the World Lost a Giant

So a great man passed away in February 2022, the legendary life success coach Bob Proctor. But "great" doesn't begin to capture what this man was. He was a force of nature, a revolutionary of the mind, a architect of human potential. His passing wasn't just news to me; it was a seismic shift in my personal universe, an emotional earthquake that left me simultaneously grief-stricken and profoundly grateful.

This was personal, deeply, intimately personal. Because I considered this man my greatest mentor, though we'd never sat across from each other over coffee, though he'd never known my name among the millions he touched. His teachings and wisdom didn't just influence my life; they rescued it, rebuilt it, and redirected it toward possibilities I couldn't have imagined from the darkness where I once dwelt. Bob Proctor was the voice that called me out of my cave of despair and into the sunlight of my own potential.

Rock Bottom Has a Basement

Let me take you back to where it all began, or rather, where everything had fallen apart. Way back in 1998, when I was 32 years of age, I was living proof that time alone doesn't heal all wounds. It had been about 15 years since I'd initially left high school, that chamber of horrors where I had been bullied quite badly. Fifteen years, and yet those wounds still bled fresh every day.

Bullying is a hard thing to cope with when you don't know how, when no one teaches you that the cruel words of others don't define your worth, when you internalize every insult until it becomes your inner dialogue. The schoolyard tormentors were long gone, but they'd taken up permanent residence in my head, their voices had become my own self-talk. Every morning, I woke up to their echoes, telling me I wasn't enough, would never be enough.

And if school was my daily battlefield, home was supposed to be my sanctuary, but it wasn't. I also had quite a troubled home life at that time, a reality that compounded the isolation and pain I felt. My family had struggled through a situation where one of my parents suffered a long-term affliction which impacted us all in profound and devastating ways. Mental illness, addiction, chronic disease, whatever form it took, it cast a shadow over our entire household, turning what should have been a refuge into another source of stress and uncertainty.

The details are less important than the impact: imagine being a young person with trouble on the home front and persecution at school, with nowhere to feel safe, nowhere to just be yourself without fear or anxiety. I'd become a bit of a lost soul, though "a bit" is perhaps the understatement of the century. I was completely, utterly lost, wandering through life without a compass, without a map, without even a destination in mind.

The Resume of a Lost Soul

I had tried, God knows I had tried. I went to university, then college, searching for something, meaning, purpose, direction, anything that might fill the emptiness inside. I tried various things in life, jumping from one pursuit to another like a drowning man grasping at pieces of driftwood. I accumulated experiences like someone collecting stamps, hoping that quantity might somehow transform into quality, that motion might somehow become progress.

I had eventually gotten some qualifications, pieces of paper that were supposed to mean something, supposed to open doors, supposed to validate my existence. But they felt hollow, meaningless. Because despite the certificates and credentials, despite the years of effort and study, I still hadn't really made anything of myself. The bullies' voices in my head reminded me daily: *You're still nothing. You're still nobody.*

At 32, here's what I had to show for my three decades on Earth: I was single, not by choice but by a crushing lack of self-worth that made me believe I had nothing to offer anyone. I had no job, not even a bad one, just an endless string of rejections and failed attempts. I had no money, not just "broke" in the casual way people say it, but genuinely, desperately penniless, counting coins for bread, avoiding phone calls from creditors, feeling the weight of financial fear every waking moment.

When the Body Breaks Down

But wait, it gets worse. As if the universe wanted to ensure I hit absolute rock bottom, I had even endured surgery of the stomach for Crohn's disease. The diagnosis came like a cruel punchline to an already tragic joke: Crohn's colitis of the bowel, an inflammatory condition that attacked my digestive system with the same relentlessness that life seemed to attack everything else about me.

The surgery was traumatic, not just physically but psychologically. There's something about being cut open, about having parts of your body removed, that makes you confront your mortality in a visceral way. The doctors, with their clinical detachment, delivered what they considered a life sentence: "You'll be on medication for the rest of your life." Pills to wake up, pills to eat, pills to sleep, pills to function, a pharmaceutical prison with no possibility of parole.

And so I was quite literally, as Bob himself would later teach me to recognize, 'unhappy, sick and broke', the terrible triad that he identified as the default state of most people who haven't learned the principles of successful living. But I wasn't just experiencing these conditions; I was drowning in them. I had become them. They weren't just my circumstances; they were my identity.

My relationships with family were dysfunctional, strained by years of unresolved pain, unspoken resentments, and the sheer exhaustion of everyone trying to survive their own struggles while living under the same roof. We were like survivors of a shipwreck, clinging to the same piece of debris but unable to help each other swim. I didn't know what to do. I didn't even know what to want to do. I was 32 years old and felt like my life was already over.

The Gift of Desperation

But here's something I've learned since then: sometimes the greatest gifts come wrapped in the ugliest packages. My surgery experience had frightened me enough to create what I now recognize as a crucial shift in my mindset. When you're lying in a hospital bed, when you've been literally cut open and sewn back together, when doctors are telling you your body is essentially broken, something happens. You either give up entirely, or something deep inside you rises up and says, "No. There has to be more than this. There has to be a way out."

I was searching for answers to life's big, nagging questions, questions that had evolved from "Why me?" to "What now?" to "How do I change this?" I was almost desperate, no, I was completely desperate, to find a way to change things, to change direction, to change myself. The pain had become unbearable, and when pain becomes unbearable, you become willing to do anything to stop it.

I asked everyone I knew for any help or advice. I swallowed my pride (what little I had left) and became that person, the one who corners you at parties asking about the meaning of life, the one who desperately seeks wisdom in fortune cookies, the one who hopes that maybe, just maybe, someone else has the answer they can't find themselves.

The Cassette Tape That Changed Everything

And then, in what seemed like an insignificant moment but would prove to be the pivotal point of my entire existence, a friend of mine, someone who had witnessed my struggle and recognized my desperation, handed me a cassette tape. Just a simple, plain cassette tape, the kind that was already becoming obsolete even in 1998. He said simply, "Try this!"

I looked at it skeptically. On side-A, it had just one word written there in plain handwriting: Attitude. On side-B, it had another one-word title: Responsibility. That was it. No fancy packaging, no professional label, no promise of miracles. Just two words that would become the foundation of my transformation.

So, I sat on my bed, my childhood bed in my little bedroom in my parents' house, the same room where I'd hidden from the world as a teenager, the same four walls that had witnessed years of tears and desperation, and I played those two sides. The tape player was old, inherited from better times, its buttons worn from years of use. The sound quality was tinny, occasionally warping. But it was enough. More than enough.

The Voice of Resistance

At first, I was very resistant to what I was hearing. These were the days before social media, before YouTube, before podcasts, when "personal development" wasn't a hashtag or a industry but something whispered about in certain circles, something vaguely suspicious and probably American. No one really talked about personal development, at least not in my world of working-class struggle and generational patterns of limitation.

My inner dialogue was immediate and harsh: *Oh my God, it's going to be an American guy,* and it was, Bob's distinctive voice filling my small room with its confidence and certainty. *He's probably going to talk about God or something. It's probably some Christian thing,* my cynicism already building walls against anything that might challenge my worldview. *Or it's Amway or something like that,* because surely there had to be a catch, a scam, a reason why this wouldn't work for someone like me.

I was very cynical, and I was very negative in my thinking, not by choice but by conditioning. Because when you've been through an awful upbringing, when lots of things have gone wrong in your young life, when you've been taught through experience that hope leads to disappointment and trust leads to betrayal, cynicism becomes your armor. Negativity becomes your protection against further hurt.

I am not blaming my parents or anything, they were doing their best with their own wounds and limitations. But the fact remained that a lot of things had gone wrong for me at home and at school, and the cumulative effect was that I simply had a very negative, cynical outlook on life. I didn't think optimistically at all. Optimism, in my experience, was for people who hadn't yet been properly introduced to reality.

The Illusion of Positivity

Here's the irony that Bob would later help me understand: I actually thought I was a positive person. Because I was very earnest about wanting to do things in my life and wanting to be happy, I confused desire with positivity. I wanted good things to happen. I hoped they would. I wished on stars and birthday candles. But as Bob would teach me, there's a massive difference between hoping and believing, between wishing and expecting.

I didn't realize that I was, as Bob would later articulate so perfectly, 'hoping positive but thinking negative.' On the surface, I'd say things like "Maybe things will get better" or "I hope something good happens," but underneath, in the depths of my subconscious mind where our real beliefs live, I was convinced that I was a hopeless case and that nothing would ever change. I was like someone standing at the edge of a cliff, saying "I hope I can fly" while being absolutely certain I would fall.

The Challenge

But something made me keep listening. Maybe it was desperation. Maybe it was having nothing left to lose. Maybe it was just the simple fact that someone had cared enough to give me this tape. I made myself listen to 'Attitude' and 'Responsibility' by Bob Proctor from his *Winners' Choice* series.

And then Bob said something on the tape that stopped me cold: "Keep listening to this twice a day, every day, for 30 days. Commit to that." It wasn't a suggestion. It wasn't a "try this if you feel like it." It was a challenge, a directive, a prescription for change. Twice a day. Every day. For 30 days. No exceptions, no excuses.

So, against every cynical bone in my body, against every voice in my head that said this was stupid and wouldn't work, I started playing it over and over. Morning and night. Before breakfast and before bed. The words began to seep into my consciousness like water into parched earth.

The Resistance from Outside

My Dad, bless him, quickly got the idea that something was going on in that bedroom of mine. The same tape playing repeatedly, the sound of Bob's voice becoming a constant presence in our small house. He was concerned, maybe even a little afraid. This wasn't normal behavior, especially not for his defeated, depressed son.

"You're brainwashing yourself with that crap," he said one day, the worry evident in his voice disguised as dismissiveness. He'd grown up in a world where you kept your head down, accepted your lot, and didn't fill your head with "American nonsense" about success and achievement.

I looked at him, my father who had worked hard all his life but never escaped the cycle of limitation, who had his own dreams crushed by his own conditioning, and something new stirred in me. Not anger, not resentment, but a quiet determination.

"Well, Dad," I said, surprised by the steadiness in my own voice, "you might think that, but you're not going to complain when you see the results."

I didn't know it then, but that was the first time I'd spoken from belief rather than hope. It was the first time I'd declared a future rather than wished for one. It was the beginning of everything.

Little did I know that this worn cassette tape, this voice from a stranger named Bob Proctor, was about to completely rewrite the story of my life. The man on the tape would become more than a teacher, he would become the catalyst for a transformation so complete that the Adrian listening in that small bedroom would soon be unrecognizable.

This was how I found Bob Proctor. Or perhaps, more accurately, this was how Bob Proctor found me, broken, desperate, and finally, finally ready to change.

LAYING THE FOUNDATIONS

A short time after I started studying the lessons on that tape, my hunger for Bob's wisdom grew exponentially. It was as though I'd discovered a hidden treasure trove, and I found myself eagerly seeking out more of his teachings. Fortune smiled upon me when a friend, recognising my newfound passion, presented me with another recording of Bob that would prove equally transformative.

In that second recording, Bob offered an analogy that would become one of the cornerstones of my understanding. He explained that learning from his teachings was rather like observing a building site in progress. The casual observer might grow impatient watching the seemingly endless months of groundwork, the careful excavation, the precise laying of foundations, the meticulous attention to what lies beneath the surface. Yet this painstaking foundation work, though it appears to move at a glacial pace, is absolutely critical. Once those foundations are properly laid, once they're solid and true, the superstructure can rise with remarkable speed, floors appearing almost overnight by comparison.

"When you're listening to this material," Bob would say in that distinctive, resonant voice of his, "you're laying the foundation. You're training your mind for an entirely new way of thinking." Those words resonated with me profoundly, for I began to understand that the repetitive listening, the daily absorption of these concepts, wasn't merely academic learning, it was mental conditioning of the deepest kind.

From Bob's tape, I learned to cultivate what he called "a good attitude", not the superficial positivity that glosses over life's challenges, but a fundamental shift in perspective that allowed me to see the inherent potential in every person I encountered. I discovered how to look for the good in everything, to seek out the silver lining in every situation, no matter how bleak it might initially appear. This wasn't about denial or wishful thinking; it was about training my mind to focus on possibilities rather than limitations, on solutions rather than problems.

Furthermore, I learned perhaps the most liberating lesson of all: to take complete responsibility for both my life and my results. Bob taught me to stop being a victim of circumstances, to cease blaming my life situations on external forces, society, the government, politicians, the economy, my parents, or even those kids at school who had made my childhood so difficult. This wasn't about letting others off the hook for their actions, but rather about reclaiming my power to shape my own destiny.

Most significantly of all, I learned that if I wanted anything, truly wanted it with every fibre of my being, and I set a clear, definite goal to achieve it, and I took complete responsibility for making that goal happen, then transformation was not only possible but inevitable. The key ingredients were persistence without exception, never giving up regardless of temporary setbacks, maintaining that good attitude even in the face of adversity, and consistently doing all the right things, day after day after day.

The beautiful truth Bob revealed was elegantly simple: if I combined burning desire with unwavering persistence, maintained the right mental attitude, and took consistent action, virtually anything could happen. This wasn't pie-in-the-sky thinking, it was a practical formula for achievement that had been proven time and again.

And pretty soon, as Bob had promised, things began to change. Not all at once, mind you, but gradually, almost imperceptibly at first. It was as though I'd planted seeds in fertile soil, and whilst I couldn't see the growth happening beneath the surface, I could sense that something fundamental was shifting within me.

Looking back now, with the clarity that only hindsight can provide, I realise that if that learning hadn't happened, if I hadn't absorbed those foundational lessons from Bob's recordings, the entire trajectory of my life would have been dramatically different. I never would have developed the confidence and mindset necessary to attract the love of my life. I never would have met my wife, that remarkable woman who would become my partner in every sense of the word. And consequently, I never would have had my children, those precious souls who have brought such joy and meaning to my existence.

The profundity of this realisation struck me most powerfully when my son Aiden was born. As I held that tiny, perfect human being in my arms for the first time, I felt an overwhelming sense of gratitude, not just for his safe arrival, but for the chain of events that had led to this moment. In a spontaneous gesture that surprised even myself, I turned to my wife and asked, "Can we give him the second name of Robert, after Bob Proctor? Robert Proctor?"

The request hung in the air for a moment. Here was a man my wife had never met, someone who existed in our lives only through his voice on recordings, yet whose influence had been so profound that I wanted to honour him in the naming of our firstborn son. Without hesitation, she agreed. She understood, perhaps better than anyone, how fundamentally Bob's teachings had transformed me and, by extension, our family's destiny.

And so he was named Aiden Robert, a name that carries within it not just our hopes and dreams for our son, but also a tribute to the man whose wisdom had made our family's existence possible.

Now Bob is gone, having left this physical plane to whatever lies beyond. Yet I find comfort in knowing that my son carries that name as a small but significant part of Bob's enduring legacy and influence in my life. Every time I speak my son's full name, I'm reminded of the debt of gratitude I owe to a man who, through the simple act of recording his thoughts and insights, provided the foundation stones upon which I was able to build not just success, but a life of meaning, purpose, and profound joy.

In this way, Bob's influence continues to ripple forward through time, touching not only my life but the life of the next generation, and perhaps the generation after that. The foundations he helped me lay all those years ago continue to support the ever-growing structure of our family's happiness, dreams, and achievements.

WRITING OUT GOALS

THE FUTURE IN THE PRESENT TENSE

A life-changing moment arrived with deceptive simplicity. It was an ordinary evening, the kind where the weight of possibilities hangs heavy in the air, when I made a decision that would fundamentally alter the trajectory of my existence. I sat down at my kitchen table with nothing more than a simple pen and a blank sheet of paper, yet what I was about to do would prove to be one of the most powerful exercises of my entire life. Following Bob's precise instructions, I decided to write a detailed description of the life I wanted to see manifesting just a few years into the future.

This wasn't to be a wish list or a collection of hopeful thoughts scribbled down in haste. This was something far more profound. I was about to write about my future as though it was already here, as though I was living it in the present moment. Bob had been very specific about this technique, emphasising that the subconscious mind responds most powerfully when we speak to it in the present tense, when we paint vivid pictures of our desired reality as though it already exists.

Taking Bob's advice to heart, I began with the transformative words he'd taught me: 'I am so happy and grateful now that I am...' These weren't just words on a page; they were incantations of possibility, declarations of intent that would resonate through every fibre of my being.

With careful deliberation, I wrote a comprehensive list of all the things I wanted to see manifesting in my future. Bob had been adamant about the importance of writing everything in very clear, specific detail. Vague aspirations, he taught, produce vague results. The subconscious mind needs precise instructions, vivid imagery, and absolute clarity about what we truly desire.

'I am so happy and grateful now that I am a teacher,' I wrote, feeling the words flow from my pen with unexpected emotion, 'with a good income that allows me to live comfortably and with dignity.' The very act of writing those words sent a thrill through me—here was a profession that would allow me to make a meaningful difference whilst providing financial security.

'I have my own house,' I continued, visualising the front door key turning in my hand, the satisfaction of ownership, the pride of having a place to truly call home. 'I am happily married to a wonderful wife who loves and supports me, and we are blessed with two beautiful children who bring joy and laughter into our lives every single day. I drive a reliable, good-quality car that gets me wherever I need to go safely and comfortably.'

But I didn't stop there. Bob had taught me that life wasn't just about meeting basic needs—it was about creating richness, fulfilment, and joy in every aspect of our existence. So I added the things that would make life truly rewarding and meaningful.

'I am now writing books,' I wrote, imagining my thoughts and insights reaching readers around the world, making a positive impact on their lives just as Bob's recordings had impacted mine. 'I am creating videos that inspire and educate others, sharing the wisdom I've gained on this incredible journey of personal transformation.'

I even included what might have seemed like trivial details to others, but which represented comfort and simple pleasures to me: 'I have a large television and collections of all my favourite programmes on DVD, so I can enjoy quality entertainment whenever I choose. Most importantly of all, I enjoy vibrant, excellent health that allows me to fully embrace every opportunity life presents.'

Page after page, I listed everything that my heart truly desired. I wrote about financial abundance, meaningful relationships, personal growth, creative expression, and the deep satisfaction that comes from living a life of purpose. Each item was written with precision, painted in vivid detail, and expressed with profound gratitude as though it had already manifested.

What happened next still astounds me to this day. Over the course of the following year, I systematically ticked off every single item on that list. Not most of them—all of them. It was as though the universe had received a detailed blueprint of my desires and set about orchestrating the circumstances necessary to bring each one into reality.

The teaching position materialised through a series of what seemed like coincidences but which I now understand were the natural result of focused intention combined with preparedness. The house became available at exactly the right time, with terms I could manage. My future wife appeared in my life when I was finally ready to recognise and appreciate true love. The children followed in perfect timing, completing our family in ways I had barely dared to imagine.

Even the seemingly smaller items manifested with precision—the car, the entertainment system, the creative outlets. Each tick mark on that original list represented not just the achievement of a goal, but confirmation that this process Bob had taught me was genuinely transformational.

Today, I'm remarkably close to having my house completely paid off—a financial milestone that once seemed impossibly distant. The contrast with my starting point is almost surreal. When I first sat down to write that list, I was absolutely flat broke. Not just financially struggling, but genuinely destitute in every sense of the word.

I was surviving on unemployment benefits, collecting what we call 'the dole'—those meagre government payments that barely keep body and soul together. Every day was a challenge just to meet basic necessities. I was living hand-to-mouth, with no prospects, no clear direction, and certainly no realistic hope of achieving the ambitious goals I would soon be writing down.

The irony of my transformation becomes even more remarkable when I consider how it all began. I didn't even purchase those life-changing recordings that started this incredible journey. A generous friend, recognising something in me that I couldn't yet see in myself, had simply handed them to me and said, "Listen to these." They cost me absolutely nothing financially, yet they helped me acquire virtually everything I wanted from life.

Those free tapes, born from one person's kindness and another's willingness to share wisdom, became the catalyst for a complete life transformation. They took me from the depths of financial despair to the heights of personal fulfilment and success. In retrospect, they represent one of the greatest investments anyone has ever made on my behalf— an investment of faith, hope, and human compassion that paid dividends beyond measure.

Bob's teaching about writing goals in the present tense hadn't just changed my circumstances; it had fundamentally altered my relationship with possibility itself. I had learned that the future isn't something that happens to us—it's something we consciously create, one carefully chosen word at a time.

HE'S GONE TO MEET HIS MENTOR

The year 2002 brought with it an opportunity I had been dreaming about ever since those first transformative recordings had changed my life. After years of listening to Bob's voice through speakers and headphones, imagining what it might be like to meet the man whose wisdom had literally rescued me from despair, I finally had my chance. A personal development convention was being held not too far from where I lived, and Bob Proctor was scheduled to be the keynote speaker.

Without hesitation, I registered for the event. This wasn't about the other speakers or the workshops on offer, this was my pilgrimage to meet the man who had become my unwitting mentor, the voice that had guided me from darkness into light.

The moment finally arrived when I found myself standing in a queue of eager admirers, each person clutching books to be signed, each with their own story of transformation to share. My heart was pounding as I approached him, this larger-than-life figure who had seemed almost mythical through his recordings, yet here he was, absolutely real, absolutely present, and absolutely approachable.

When my turn came, I stepped forward and extended my hand to shake his. The moment our hands connected, I felt a surge of emotion that surprised me with its intensity. Here was the man whose words had literally saved my life, whose teachings had pulled me back from the brink of hopelessness and shown me a path to prosperity and fulfilment.

"Thank you," I managed to say, my voice slightly trembling with emotion, "thank you for everything you've done for me. Your teachings really changed my life, completely and utterly transformed everything about my circumstances and my future."

Bob's response was immediate and genuine. His face lit up with that warm, encouraging smile I had somehow sensed even through his audio recordings. He wasn't just going through the motions of meeting fans; he was genuinely interested, genuinely pleased to hear about the positive impact his work had made. He was such a gracious man, so warm and generous with his time, someone who seemed to carry within him an inexhaustible supply of encouraging words for everyone he encountered.

Throughout the day, I watched in fascination as person after person approached Bob, each sharing their dreams, their goals, their aspirations for the future. His response was remarkably consistent and delivered with absolute conviction: "You can do it." These weren't empty platitudes or polite encouragements, when Bob said those words, you believed them. There was something in his voice, his presence, his absolute certainty that made you feel as though your dreams weren't just possible, but inevitable.

I particularly remember one lady who approached him during a break between sessions. She seemed nervous, hesitant, as she shared her business aspirations with him. When she finished speaking, she asked him directly, "Mr. Proctor, do you have a job?"

His response brought laughter rippling through the small crowd that had gathered around him: "No," he said with that characteristic twinkle in his eye, "I've been too busy making money to have a job."

It was a perfect Bob Proctor moment, simultaneously humorous and profoundly instructive. Here was a man who had transcended the traditional employee mindset entirely, who had learned to create wealth rather than simply exchange time for money. In that one sentence, he encapsulated everything he taught about thinking beyond conventional limitations.

Although I was still in the relatively early stages of my personal transformation journey and continued to struggle with crippling shyness and self-esteem issues that occasionally surfaced despite my progress, Bob seemed remarkably tolerant and encouraging towards me, just as he was with everyone else. There was no judgment in his eyes, no impatience with my occasionally stumbling words or nervous energy. He possessed that rare quality of making each person feel as though they were the most important individual in the room during their brief interaction with him.

When Bob took to the stage for his main presentation, the atmosphere in the auditorium was electric with anticipation. What followed was one of the most fascinating and enlightening talks I had ever witnessed. He spoke with passion and clarity about levels of awareness, how our consciousness operates at different altitudes, and how each level we ascend allows us to see further, understand more, and achieve things that would have been impossible from our previous vantage point.

"Raise your level of awareness," he emphasised, and those words became seared into my memory as one of the key takeaways from that entire experience. It wasn't enough, he explained, to simply want more or to work harder within our current level of thinking. Real transformation required us to elevate our consciousness itself, to literally become more aware beings capable of perceiving opportunities and solutions that were invisible to us before.

This concept revolutionised my understanding of personal development. It wasn't just about positive thinking or goal-setting, though those were important tools. It was about fundamentally expanding the capacity of our minds to comprehend and create reality at higher levels.

So it fills me with profound sadness to know that Bob has now passed away, leaving this physical realm to reunite with his own mentor, Napoleon Hill, in whatever dimension awaits us beyond this life. Yet even in my grief, I find tremendous comfort knowing that his teachings continue to ripple outward, touching new lives every single day.

What a remarkably generous man he was, not just in person but throughout his entire career! In the years following our meeting, Bob embraced the digital age with enthusiasm, placing enormous amounts of his wisdom and teachings on the Internet completely free of charge. Videos, articles, courses, he seemed determined to make his life's work accessible to anyone, regardless of their financial circumstances.

It was as though he understood that his true legacy wouldn't be measured in book sales or seminar attendance, but in the number of lives transformed, the amount of human potential unleashed, and the ripple effects of positive change that would continue long after he was gone.

Bob Proctor didn't just teach success principles, he embodied them. He didn't just talk about generosity, he lived it. And while we mourn his passing, we can celebrate the fact that his voice, his wisdom, and his transformational teachings will continue to guide seekers toward their highest potential for generations to come.

Somewhere, I like to imagine, he's having the most extraordinary conversation with Napoleon Hill, comparing notes on the countless lives they've touched and planning new ways to inspire human beings to reach for the stars. The student has become the teacher, and now both mentors continue their work from a realm where limitations no longer exist.

HOW BOB PROCTOR FACED DEATH

One aspect of Bob Proctor's character that continues to fascinate and inspire me is the extraordinary way he approached the end of his physical life, a perspective that stood in stark contrast to how most people in our society view mortality.

There's something peculiar about the human condition, something almost programmed into our collective consciousness by the world we inhabit, that compels us to regard death with overwhelming sadness and dread. From childhood onwards, we're conditioned through cultural narratives, religious teachings, and social expectations to think of death as the ultimate tragedy, the final defeat, the most sorrowful event that can befall any human being.

Yet Bob Proctor viewed this universal human experience through an entirely different lens, one that revealed not fear but fascination, not despair but anticipation. Death, to Bob, wasn't something to be dreaded or avoided at all costs. Instead, he regarded it with genuine curiosity and excitement, believing that the transition from physical to spiritual existence represented one of the most intriguing adventures a soul could embark upon.

"Something exciting is probably going to happen," he would say when discussing the topic, his eyes lighting up with the same enthusiasm he brought to discussing business principles or success strategies. This wasn't denial or bravado, it was a deeply held philosophical conviction rooted in his understanding of the nature of existence itself.

Bob held the profound belief that we are fundamentally spiritual beings temporarily housed in physical bodies, rather than physical beings occasionally experiencing spiritual moments. From this perspective, death wasn't an ending but a homecoming, a return to our natural state of pure consciousness, unencumbered by the limitations and constraints of physical form.

He often spoke about his eagerness to enter what he called "the spiritual realm," approaching it with the same intellectual curiosity that a scientist might bring to exploring an uncharted territory. What would it be like to exist as pure consciousness? What mysteries would be revealed? What expanded awareness would become possible when freed from the confines of flesh and bone?

Bob lived to the age of 87, a long life by most standards, yet throughout his final years, he displayed a remarkable absence of the fear that typically accompanies advancing age. While many people become increasingly anxious about mortality as they grow older, Bob seemed to become more fascinated by the prospect of what lay beyond the physical realm.

This fearless approach to death stemmed partly from one of his core philosophical principles: the law of polarity, which states that everything contains its opposite. "You cannot have a bad without a good," he would explain with characteristic clarity. If death appears to be something negative, then according to universal law, there must be something equally positive about it that we're simply not seeing from our limited perspective.

When applied to someone who has been suffering, whether from illness, pain, or life circumstances, we can often identify the good quite readily: "At least their suffering is over," we say, recognising the relief that comes with the end of physical or emotional torment. But Bob's understanding went deeper than this surface-level comfort.

I believe Bob's peaceful relationship with mortality also stemmed from the extraordinary life of fulfilment and success he had lived. This wasn't a man approaching death with a heavy heart full of regrets, lamenting missed opportunities or unexpressed dreams. He wasn't someone lying on his deathbed thinking, "Good grief, I'm going to die now, and I've never accomplished anything I truly wanted to do."

In the most profound sense, Bob hadn't taken his music to the grave. That beautiful metaphor speaks to those tragic figures who die with their songs unsung, their books unwritten, their dreams unexpressed, their potential unrealised. Bob had spent decades sharing his gifts with the world, touching millions of lives, and expressing his unique talents to their fullest extent.

He had built businesses, written books, delivered countless seminars, mentored thousands of students, and created a legacy of wisdom that would continue influencing people for generations to come. He had loved deeply, lived fully, and given generously of his time, knowledge, and resources. When he looked back over his 87 years, he could do so with satisfaction rather than sorrow.

This absence of regret created a remarkable freedom in his final years. He wasn't tormented by thoughts of "I wish I'd done this" or "If only I'd pursued that opportunity" or "Why didn't I tell that person how I felt?" Instead, he could approach the end of his physical journey with a sense of completion, knowing that he had squeezed every drop of potential from his time on Earth.

There's something profoundly instructive about Bob's approach to mortality, this combination of philosophical acceptance, spiritual curiosity, and life-completion satisfaction. He faced death not as a defeat but as a graduation ceremony, not as an ending but as a commencement, not as something to be feared but as the ultimate adventure in consciousness.

While he obviously loved life and embraced every moment of his physical existence with passion and enthusiasm, he remained free from the paralysing fear that grips so many people when they contemplate their own mortality. This freedom allowed him to live more fully in his final years, to continue teaching and inspiring others right up until the end, and to model for all of us what it looks like to approach death with dignity, curiosity, and peaceful acceptance.

Perhaps most remarkably of all, Bob's fearless approach to death enhanced rather than diminished his appreciation for life. When you're not constantly worried about when your time will end, you're free to focus completely on making the most of the time you have. In this way, Bob's philosophy about death became yet another tool for living more successfully, more fully, and more joyfully in the present moment.

His legacy includes not just the principles he taught about success and prosperity, but also this profound lesson about how to face our own mortality with grace, curiosity, and an unshakeable faith in the continuity of consciousness. In teaching us how to live well, Bob Proctor also taught us how to die well, and perhaps that's one of the greatest gifts any teacher can offer their students.

A PATHWAY OUT OF THE DARKNESS

I really was in a very dark place before I discovered Bob Proctor's teachings back in the late 1990s. The description "dark place" hardly does justice to the psychological abyss I had fallen into, a suffocating pit of despair where hope seemed like a foreign concept and the future appeared to hold nothing but more of the same grinding misery.

The 1980s and 1990s had been brutal decades for me personally, years that felt like an endless gauntlet of challenges and heartbreak. My mother had been gravely ill for extended periods, her condition casting a pall of worry and helplessness over our entire family. Meanwhile, my father had been away at work constantly, his absence during these difficult times leaving me feeling isolated and unsupported just when I needed stability most.

School, which should have been a refuge from home troubles, instead became another theatre of torment. I was systematically bullied by classmates who seemed to take perverse pleasure in targeting someone who was already struggling. Day after day, I would face the humiliation and cruelty that only children can inflict upon one another, whilst simultaneously worrying about my mother's health and missing my father's presence.

My home life had deteriorated into what I can only describe as a long, dark struggle, a seemingly endless period where joy was rare, laughter was scarce, and each day felt like an exercise in mere survival rather than living. I was trapped in a cycle of negativity that seemed to feed upon itself, growing stronger and more consuming with each passing week.

The significant breakthrough that occurred when I first listened to Bob Proctor was nothing short of revelatory. As his words penetrated my consciousness, I began to realise with startling clarity that I had been dwelling obsessively on negative thoughts and experiences. Like a person picking at a wound, I had been mentally rehearsing every slight, every disappointment, every fear and frustration until they had become the dominant themes of my inner life.

This constant focus on negativity wasn't just making me sad, it was actively depressing me, bringing me down to depths I hadn't even known existed, and creating a sense of frustration about life that coloured every interaction and every possibility with shades of grey and black.

One of Bob's key principles became the turning point in my transformation: "Take your mind off all of the things that you don't want and focus exclusively on the things you do want." These words hit me like a bolt of lightning, illuminating a path I hadn't even known existed.

I remember the moment this concept truly clicked for me, it was as though someone had suddenly switched on a light in a room where I'd been stumbling around in darkness for years. I discovered that when I deliberately redirected my attention away from my problems and towards my possibilities, something miraculous began to happen.

If I focused solely on what I wanted rather than what I was trying to escape, suddenly all of those heavy, unhappy feelings that had been my constant companions simply began to dissolve. It wasn't gradual, it was almost immediate. When the barrage of unhappy thoughts finally subsided, I actually started to feel genuinely good for the first time in years.

This wasn't just the absence of negative feelings; it was the presence of something positive and energising. Focusing on my desires had me looking towards the future with anticipation rather than dread, thinking about possibilities rather than limitations, imagining scenarios where I was thriving rather than merely surviving.

Bob taught that once you begin focusing on and truly thinking about the things you want in life, you naturally start moving towards them. This isn't mystical thinking, it's practical psychology. When your mind is focused on a destination, your subconscious begins working to identify opportunities, resources, and pathways that will help you reach that destination.

What fascinated me most was Bob's observation that most people don't even acknowledge what they really want. They've become so convinced that their dreams are impossible, so certain that their desires are unrealistic, that they refuse to admit to themselves what they actually want to have, achieve, or become.

"Oh, it's unrealistic," they tell themselves, shutting down their dreams before they've even given them a proper chance to breathe. This self-imposed limitation becomes a prison of their own making, keeping them trapped in lives that fall far short of their potential.

Even when people do acknowledge what they truly want, Bob noted, most of them fail to take the crucial next step: they don't set their desires as concrete goals and write them down. Instead, these dreams remain vague thoughts floating around in the back of their minds like background music, present but not commanding attention.

They think to themselves, "Well, I'd really like to do this, and I'd really like to have that," but they never actually pick up a pen and paper and write it down as a formal declaration: "This is my goal. This is what I'm committed to achieving."

Most people don't think of goal-setting as something that ordinary individuals do, they see it as something reserved for business executives or professional athletes. But Bob taught me that this is actually one of the most powerful tools available to anyone willing to use it.

The research backs this up completely: studies have consistently shown that people who write down their goals are significantly more likely to achieve them than those who merely think about what they want. The simple act of putting pen to paper transforms a wish into a commitment, a dream into a plan.

Look at any successful entity, governments, corporations, championship sports teams, and you'll find they all follow the same practice: they write down their objectives clearly and specifically. We should follow their example because it works, regardless of whether we're trying to run a country, build a business, or simply improve our personal lives.

However, Bob identified the biggest obstacle that stops people from pursuing their dreams: the paralysing belief that they need to know "how" before they can begin. This is the really, truly important barrier that keeps people stuck in lives they don't want.

"I have a goal, I want to do this," they think, "but I don't know how to achieve it." They convince themselves that without a detailed roadmap, without knowing every step of the journey in advance, they're doomed to failure. "I guess I'm screwed," becomes their default response to any ambitious aspiration.

Bob's answer to this limitation was beautifully illustrated through the story of Sir Edmund Hillary and his conquest of Mount Everest. Hillary had absolutely no idea how to reach the summit when he first set his goal. The route was uncharted, the challenges were unknown, and the obstacles were largely unimaginable.

Bob would tell the story with obvious relish: how Hillary and his team tried and failed, tried and failed again, each attempt teaching them something new about the mountain's demands and their own capabilities. Finally, after persistent effort and accumulated learning, they tried and succeeded, planting their flag on the highest point on Earth.

The process was purely exploratory. Hillary had a crystal-clear goal: to stand on top of that mountain, to plant the flag, to conquer Everest. That vision was seared into his imagination, he could see himself achieving it, feel the satisfaction of accomplishment, experience the triumph in vivid detail.

But the crucial point, the key takeaway that Bob emphasised repeatedly, was that Hillary didn't let not knowing how stop him from trying. He understood intuitively what many people never grasp: that the "how" reveals itself through action, not contemplation.

Like an explorer moving through uncharted territory with only a torch to light the path immediately ahead, Hillary worked out the route to his goal bit by bit, step by step, revelation by revelation. He found the way to his objective gradually, through trial and error, through persistence and adaptation.

This is how all meaningful achievement works, Bob taught me. You don't need to see the entire staircase to take the first step. You identify the first small distance in front of you and move that distance. Once you've covered that ground, you can see the next portion of the journey more clearly.

The path is rarely straight. Maybe you go left, then right, then up and down. Maybe there are obstacles that force you to find creative detours. Maybe there are setbacks that require you to retreat temporarily before finding a new approach.

But this is where persistence becomes your most valuable asset, where your human inventiveness in overcoming challenges proves its worth. Each obstacle becomes a puzzle to solve rather than a reason to quit. Each setback becomes information to use rather than evidence that you should abandon your dreams.

The beautiful truth that Bob revealed is that you don't need to know how to achieve your goal when you begin, you will learn how through the process of pursuing it. The knowledge, the skills, the connections, the opportunities will all present themselves as you move forward with faith and determination.

When you finally reach your goal, when you achieve what once seemed impossible, that's when you'll be able to look back and see the complete picture. "Oh, now I can see how I got here," you'll say to yourself, marvelling at the journey that seemed so mysterious when you began.

But you don't know how when you start, and that's perfectly fine. Don't let not knowing how to achieve your goal make you afraid. Don't let uncertainty become an excuse for inaction.

Don't say, "I really want to produce a motion picture for the cinema, but I don't know how," and let that ignorance stop you. Don't think, "I really want to sell a million books, but I don't know how," and abandon the dream before you've even tried. Don't tell yourself, "I really want to be a world-class athlete, but I don't know how," and settle for mediocrity as a result.

Whether your goal is to make a million pounds, to write a bestselling novel, to build a successful business, or to make a positive impact on the world, the same principle applies: set the goal clearly, commit to it completely, and start moving towards it with faith and determination.

The "how" will be revealed as you go. You will discover the way through experience, through experimentation, through the accumulation of small victories and the wisdom gained from temporary defeats. You simply must have faith in the process, trust in your ability to figure things out along the way, and refuse to give up when the path becomes difficult.

That's what I learned from Bob Proctor, and it changed everything for me. I set the big goals, the seemingly impossible goals that would have terrified the person I was before I discovered Bob's teachings. Goals that seemed crazy, unrealistic, beyond my reach.

And you know what? I made it to where I am today, which is a hell of a lot better than where I was when I started this journey. The contrast is so dramatic that sometimes I feel like I'm living someone else's life, except this life is mine, earned through the application of principles that Bob Proctor taught me during my darkest hours.

The pathway out of darkness wasn't just about changing my circumstances, it was about changing my thinking, my focus, my relationship with possibility itself. Bob didn't just teach me how to set goals; he taught me how to believe in my ability to achieve them, regardless of how impossible they might initially appear.

AND THEN THERE WAS THE SECRET

One of the pivotal moments that catapulted Bob Proctor from respected personal development teacher to global phenomenon was his prominent role in the groundbreaking film *The Secret*. This documentary, which introduced millions of people worldwide to the concept of the law of attraction, would become one of the most talked-about and controversial self-help phenomena of the 21st century.

The Secret, of course, centres entirely around the law of attraction, the idea that our thoughts, feelings, and beliefs literally attract corresponding experiences into our lives. According to this principle, we are like human magnets, constantly drawing towards us people, circumstances, and opportunities that match our dominant mental and emotional patterns.

When *The Secret* was released, it created an immediate cultural earthquake. The film spread like wildfire across the globe, shared from person to person, downloaded millions of times, and discussed in living rooms, offices, and coffee shops everywhere. But alongside the enthusiasm and life-changing testimonials came a tidal wave of criticism from mainstream media and academic circles.

Sceptics emerged from every corner, journalists, scientists, and self-appointed debunkers who questioned whether the entire concept of the law of attraction was genuinely real or merely an elaborate collection of pseudoscientific rubbish designed to separate gullible people from their money. Television programmes dedicated entire segments to "exposing" the film, newspapers published scathing reviews, and online forums buzzed with heated debates between believers and sceptics.

But here's what I can tell you from personal experience: I've actually lived through those exact situations described in *The Secret*. Not once, not twice, but repeatedly throughout my journey of applying Bob Proctor's teachings.

These are those almost mystical moments where you conceive an idea, perhaps during a quiet moment of reflection, maybe while listening to one of Bob's recordings, or possibly during a period of deep contemplation about your future. You take this idea and fix it firmly in your mind, giving it substance and detail through focused attention.

Perhaps you write about it meticulously on paper, crafting detailed descriptions of what you want to achieve or acquire. Maybe you even create what's known as a vision board, a carefully constructed collage of images, words, and symbols representing your desired outcome. You might cut out pictures from magazines, print photographs from the internet, or even draw sketches of your goal, arranging them all in a prominent place where you'll see them daily.

Then comes the crucial part: you really think about this goal intensely, focusing on it with laser-like concentration for days at a time. Or perhaps you maintain this focus for weeks, even months, returning to your vision again and again, feeling the emotions associated with achieving it, imagining yourself living the reality you've created in your mind.

And then, almost without warning, something extraordinary happens! An event occurs that seems like the most incredible coincidence imaginable, something so perfectly timed, so precisely aligned with your desires, that it brings you dramatically closer to receiving exactly what you've been visualising.

The phone rings with an unexpected opportunity. You bump into exactly the right person at exactly the right moment. A door opens that you didn't even know existed. Information comes to you from an unlikely source. Resources appear from unexpected quarters. The very thing you've been focusing on manifests in ways you could never have orchestrated through conscious effort alone.

Now, when these seemingly miraculous events occur, people tend to fall into two distinct camps of explanation, each with passionate advocates on both sides.

The first group, typically comprising the more scientifically minded individuals, will dismiss these occurrences with rational explanations: "Well, that's simply goal setting in action," they'll say with confident authority. "When something amazing appears to happen, it's merely coincidence, a fortunate alignment of circumstances. You've programmed the idea into your subconscious mind, which has then caused you to notice opportunities and take actions that make your goal more likely to manifest. It's psychology, not magic."

On the other side, you have those who embrace Bob Proctor's more metaphysical explanations with equal conviction. "What Bob teaches is absolutely correct," they'll insist with passionate certainty. "It's the power of your thoughts in action! When you hold an idea consistently in your mind, you're generating cosmic waves of energy that penetrate all time and space. These thought-waves act like a magnet, literally attracting people, circumstances, and opportunities that align with your mental image. The vision in your head possesses the power to draw the necessary elements towards you to help bring your dreams into physical reality."

But here's my perspective after years of experiencing both the process and the results: I honestly don't think it matters which explanation is correct. Why should we agonise over the mechanics when we can simply appreciate and utilise the results?

Consider this: I don't understand how an internal combustion engine works, not really. I know my car possesses one somewhere under the bonnet, and I understand that when I insert the key and turn it, the engine starts and the vehicle moves. I don't need to be a mechanical engineer to benefit from this technology, I simply accept that it works and use it to get where I need to go.

Similarly, I don't comprehend the intricate workings of the internet. I have a general understanding that there's something involving signals bouncing off satellites, vast networks of interconnected computers, hard drives storing information, and countless electronic components working in harmony. But I'm certainly not an Information Technology expert, and I don't need to be one to send emails, browse websites, or video chat with people on the other side of the world.

The same principle applies to virtually every technology we use daily. Give a smartphone or tablet to a child, and they'll instinctively turn it on and begin using it effectively within minutes. They don't need a degree in computer science or electronics, they simply accept that the device works and explore its capabilities through experimentation and play.

This pragmatic approach extends to the law of attraction as well. Rather than getting caught up in endless debates about whether it's "real" in some scientific sense, or whether it can be explained through conventional psychology, I've chosen to focus on what I know beyond any doubt: it works.

So my recommendation is beautifully simple: just do it. Just use the process, regardless of how you choose to explain it.

Pick up a pen and write down precisely what you want, in vivid detail. Describe not just the outcome but how achieving it will make you feel, what it will mean for your life, how it will impact the people you care about.

Gather pictures representing your desires and create a vision board that speaks to your deepest aspirations. Place it somewhere you'll see it daily, perhaps beside your bed, on your office wall, or on your refrigerator door. Look at these images regularly, not just with your eyes but with your imagination and emotions fully engaged.

Get genuinely emotionally involved in your vision. Feel the excitement, the gratitude, the satisfaction as though your goal has already been achieved. As Bob would say, get on the right vibration, tune in to the right frequency.

Align your thoughts, feelings, and expectations with what you truly want rather than what you fear or what seems "realistic" based on current circumstances. Focus your mental and emotional energy like a laser beam on your desired outcome.

When you do this consistently and with genuine feeling, you'll be amazed at what the universe, or your subconscious mind, or cosmic forces, or simple coincidence, call it whatever makes you comfortable, will deliver to your doorstep.

Whether this process works through goal-setting psychology and heightened awareness, or whether it operates through some deeper law of attraction that science hasn't yet fully understood, I'm genuinely not here to argue with anyone about the mechanisms involved.

What I am here to tell you, based on years of personal experience and observation, is that it works. The process produces results that seem to defy rational explanation, results that have transformed not just my own life but the lives of countless others who've had the courage to suspend their disbelief and simply try it.

In the end, perhaps Bob Proctor's greatest gift wasn't just teaching us about the law of attraction, it was showing us that we don't need to understand everything in order to benefit from it. Sometimes, the wisest approach is to stop analysing and start applying, to cease debating and begin doing.

The universe, it seems, is far more interested in our willingness to participate than in our ability to explain how the magic happens.

LIFE CHANGING

Perhaps it might help if I share some deeply personal details from my own transformation journey, because sometimes the most profound truths are found not in abstract principles but in the lived experience of real people who've walked the path from despair to triumph.

So let's talk about the most obvious and measurable indicator of change: money. When I first discovered Bob Proctor's teachings in 1998, I was in a financial state that could only be described as absolutely, utterly, catastrophically broke.

I wasn't just experiencing temporary cash flow problems or going through a rough patch, I was literally surviving on unemployment benefits. I was what we call "on the dole" or welfare, existing on those meagre government payments that barely keep you housed and fed. I had nothing, absolutely nothing, financially speaking. My bank account was a blank slate, my pockets were empty, and my financial prospects appeared non-existent.

But the money situation was merely the tip of the iceberg. My entire life was a comprehensive disaster area across every conceivable dimension. I had no girlfriend, no romantic prospects, no meaningful relationships that brought joy or companionship to my days. I had no job, no career path, no professional identity that gave me purpose or direction. I had no money, as I've mentioned, but beyond that, I had no financial literacy, no understanding of how wealth was created or sustained.

Perhaps most devastatingly of all, I had no happiness, that fundamental sense of contentment and optimism that makes life worth living had been completely drained from my existence. I had no health to speak of, my physical condition reflecting the mental and emotional neglect I'd subjected myself to for years. Everything about my life felt broken, hopeless, and heading in the wrong direction.

The particularly painful irony of my situation was that this comprehensive failure seemed to contradict everything about my earlier potential. When I was a boy in school, I had actually been known for being exceptionally imaginative and creative. Teachers, friends, and family members had regularly told me encouraging things about my abilities and prospects. I was the kid who could tell elaborate stories, who came up with original ideas, who seemed destined for some kind of creative success.

So it felt profoundly strange and deeply disheartening to find myself, years later, with absolutely nothing meaningful to do with my life except collect unemployment benefits and pursue studies in subjects that interested me intellectually but hadn't translated into any practical career opportunities. I had somehow managed to waste all that early promise and potential, ending up as a statistic rather than a success story.

When I began listening to Bob Proctor's teachings, one of the concepts that he impressed most powerfully upon my mind was revolutionary in its simplicity: you can do anything, you can have anything, literally anything you want from this world. This wasn't motivational fluff or empty encouragement; this was a fundamental truth about the nature of reality and opportunity.

Bob taught me that we live in a world where there is sufficient opportunity for everyone, regardless of their starting point or current circumstances. There's so much opportunity available in this world that you couldn't possibly take advantage of all the possibilities that surround you right now, in this very moment.

Think about it: if you had ten lifetimes to live, if you could somehow extend your existence to one hundred lifetimes, if medical science advanced to the point where you could live to be a thousand years old, you still could not exhaust all the opportunities that exist in your immediate environment today. The sheer abundance of possibility is staggering when you really contemplate it.

This realisation means that thinking in terms of lack and limitation isn't just unproductive, it's completely divorced from reality. We live in a world of abundant opportunity, surrounded by nearly eight billion people. Every single one of those people wants things, needs things, desires things, and therefore every one of those people represents potential opportunity for someone willing to serve their needs.

All human service, all business, all value creation is fundamentally about doing things for other people, solving their problems, fulfilling their desires, making their lives better in some way. If there are over seven billion potential customers or clients in the world—people who want things, who need things, who are willing to pay for solutions, then that represents an almost incomprehensible amount of opportunity, doesn't it?

The key insight Bob shared was that all you really need to do is decide: what do you actually want? What do you truly desire for your life?

You need to be completely honest with yourself about this question. You must really look into your own heart, past the layers of conditioning, past the voices of doubt and limitation, past the fear of disappointment. In your heart of hearts, that's where all the real answers are waiting to be discovered.

The solutions to your life aren't "out there" somewhere in the external world. Don't waste your time waiting for the government to solve your problems, or for society to change in ways that benefit you, or for the economy to improve, or for the right politician to be elected, or for whatever external circumstances you think need to align before you can pursue your dreams.

Those external factors are only truly relevant during genuine crises, wars, natural disasters, economic collapses, or other catastrophic events that fundamentally disrupt the normal functioning of society. Certainly, such circumstances can create significant challenges that must be navigated carefully.

But here's the crucial point: when things are generally stable and functioning normally, as they are for most people, particularly those living in western civilised parts of the world, then the only thing standing between you and your dreams is your own decision-making process. All you need to decide is what you actually, genuinely, wholeheartedly want for your life.

History is filled with examples of people who overcame terrible starting situations, who escaped from oppressive circumstances, who moved to entirely different parts of the world where they found new opportunities and created successful lives for themselves. Human beings possess an extraordinary capacity for adaptation, creativity, and persistence when they're truly committed to changing their circumstances.

So it all comes down to this fundamental question: What do you really want?

I decided what I wanted, and, following Bob's advice, I wrote it down. This simple act would prove to be one of the most transformative decisions of my entire life.

One of the concepts that Bob emphasised repeatedly, and which proved absolutely crucial to my transformation, was the extraordinary power of actually writing things down. "Don't just think it, ink it," became my personal motto. Write it down, make it tangible, give your dreams physical form on paper.

You've probably heard the saying "the pen is mightier than the sword," and perhaps dismissed it as just another cliché. You might have thought, "Yeah, okay, it's just a pen, maybe you could poke a swordsman in the eye with it," and left it at that.

But consider the deeper truth embedded in that ancient wisdom. If I'm in a position of authority, holding a pen and a piece of paper that says "this person shall be executed," then that pen wields tremendous power indeed. A swordsman might be able to execute one person through physical force, but with a pen, I could sign a document ordering the execution of a thousand people simultaneously. Conversely, I could sign a pardon that releases and frees a thousand prisoners with a single signature.

When you go to the bank and they write out a cheque or bank draft, the difference between writing the correct amount and an incorrect amount might be a single zero. Leave off that zero, and you've written a completely different sum. Add the proper zeros, and you've created the exact amount you intended. That small difference in ink can represent thousands or even millions of pounds.

The pen truly is extraordinarily powerful when you understand how to use it properly.

Think about how successful entities operate: governments, major corporations, championship sports teams. They don't just have vague goals floating around in people's minds. They have detailed plans, comprehensive strategies, specific targets, and measurable objectives. Everything is written down, typed up, documented, and distributed to everyone involved in the organisation.

Everyone knows exactly what they're supposed to be doing because it's all been written down and communicated clearly. Yet most of us go through our personal lives as though they're completely random, making decisions on the fly, hoping everything will somehow work out fine without any real planning or intentional direction.

I decided to approach my life with the same systematic planning that successful organisations use. I sat down with a pen and paper, and I wrote out the critical decisions facing me: "Should I do this or should I do that?" I created detailed lists of pros and cons for each option, examining them rationally and thoroughly. I added up all the factors, weighed the potential outcomes, and made good decisions based on clear thinking rather than emotional impulse. Those carefully considered decisions changed the entire course of my life.

I wrote down concrete ideas for goals and achievements I wanted to pursue. I didn't just think about them vaguely, I gave them specific form and substance on paper.

I wrote that I wanted to become a teacher, envisioning myself making a positive difference in young people's lives whilst earning a stable, respectable income. I wanted to get an actor's agent, opening doors to creative opportunities in film and television. I wanted to buy a good camera and explore filmmaking, expressing my creativity through visual storytelling. I wanted to put on theatrical productions, bringing stories to life on stage. I wanted to write short stories that would entertain and inspire readers. I wanted to write a full-length book that would share valuable insights with a wider audience.

On the personal side, I wrote that I wanted to get married to someone who would be my true partner in life, someone who would love and support me whilst allowing me to love and support her in return. I wanted to have two children who would bring joy and meaning to our family. I wanted to own a house that would be our sanctuary and home base. I wanted to accumulate enough money in the bank to pay off that house completely within a specific time frame, achieving true financial security.

I wrote it all out methodically, thinking carefully about my future rather than just drifting along hoping for the best. But here's the crucial detail: I didn't write these goals as though I wanted them immediately. Instead, I thought two years ahead, added two years to my current age, and projected myself forward in time. I began writing about how I wanted my life to be two years from that moment.

This time-based approach was revolutionary for me. Suddenly, I knew exactly what I was working towards for the next two years. I had a clear destination, a specific target, a detailed vision of where I wanted to be when that future date arrived.

I began working with Bob's principle that if we make firm, unequivocal decisions about what we want, and then take absolute, 100% responsibility for making those things happen—no matter what obstacles arise, no matter what setbacks occur, no matter what external circumstances try to derail us, we will inevitably make our goals reality.

Certainly, unexpected events and challenges will occasionally arise that can cause temporary problems or force us to adjust our approach. But if we remain persistent, if we continue taking complete responsibility for our results, and if we keep adapting our methods while staying focused on our ultimate objectives, we will overcome whatever difficulties attempt to knock us off course.

The formula is elegantly simple: clarity about what you want, complete responsibility for making it happen, and persistent action regardless of temporary setbacks. Follow this approach consistently, and you will achieve your goals. You will succeed beyond most people's expectations or belief.

So don't simply take my word for these principles, try them yourself. Conduct your own experiment with the power of written goals and persistent action.

Pick up a pen and paper right now, and begin thinking seriously about what you really want your life to be like a couple of years from today. Start writing it down in specific detail, creating concrete goals and actionable plans. Make a firm decision that you will make these things happen regardless of what challenges arise.

Commit to never giving up, to persisting through every setback, to maintaining your determination no matter what life throws at you. Decide that you will beat resistance with your persistence, that you will turn obstacles into stepping stones, that you will find a way around, over, under, or through any barrier that stands between you and your dreams.

Do this consistently and with genuine commitment, and I guarantee you will achieve goals that seem impossible from your current vantage point. You will experience success that goes beyond other people's belief systems about what's possible. People will look at you with amazement and ask, "How did you do that? You of all people! How did you manage to achieve something so extraordinary?"

And you'll be able to tell them with quiet confidence, "I've been working with a secret, but it's been happening on the inside, in my thoughts, my decisions, my commitment, and my persistent action."

You can do this. You have everything within you right now that you need to transform your life completely. That's what I learned from Bob Proctor, and it's what I'm sharing with you now: if someone like me, starting from absolute rock bottom, with no money, no prospects, and no apparent advantages, can completely turn their life around, then so can you.

The only question remaining is: will you pick up that pen and begin writing your new future today?

Good luck, though I suspect that once you begin applying these principles consistently, you'll discover that luck has very little to do with it.

VALE

As I bring this reflection to a close, I'm filled with profound gratitude for a man whose voice reached across time and space to transform not just my life, but countless others around the world. Bob Proctor has touched so many lives in such deeply positive ways that his influence has become immeasurable, creating ripple effects that will continue expanding outward for generations to come.

Through his recordings, his books, his seminars, and his unwavering commitment to sharing transformational wisdom, Bob became the mentor that millions of people never knew they needed. He spoke to the broken-hearted and showed them how to heal. He reached out to the financially desperate and taught them how to create abundance. He connected with those who felt trapped by circumstances and revealed the keys to their liberation.

For someone like me, lost in darkness, consumed by limitation, convinced that my circumstances were permanent, Bob's teachings were nothing short of miraculous. He didn't just offer hope; he provided a proven roadmap from despair to triumph, from poverty to prosperity, from isolation to fulfilment.

The man who gave me those life-changing recordings all those years ago probably had no idea that he was handing me the blueprint for a completely transformed existence. Bob's voice, captured on those tapes, became the catalyst for everything good that followed in my life, my career, my marriage, my children, my sense of purpose and meaning.

But my story is just one among millions. Across the globe, there are countless individuals whose lives have been fundamentally altered by Bob's wisdom. Business leaders who built empires using his principles. Artists who found the courage to pursue their dreams. Parents who broke cycles of limitation to give their children better lives. Teachers, healers, inventors, and dreamers, all carrying forward the flame of possibility that Bob helped kindle within them.

Even now, years after our last conversation, decades after I first heard his voice on those precious recordings, Bob's teachings continue to guide my decisions and shape my perspective. His principles have become so integrated into my thinking that they feel less like learned concepts and more like natural instincts.

When challenges arise, I hear his voice reminding me to focus on what I want rather than what I fear. When opportunities appear, I remember his lessons about taking responsibility and acting with persistence. When doubt creeps in, his words about the abundance of possibility help restore my faith in what's achievable.

So thank you, Bob. Thank you for being the great mentor I desperately needed during the darkest period of my life. Thank you for your generosity in sharing wisdom that could have remained private. Thank you for your persistence in spreading these transformational principles even when others doubted or criticised. Thank you for believing in human potential when many had given up on themselves.

Thank you for showing me that circumstances are temporary but the power to change them is permanent. Thank you for teaching me that the size of our problems is nothing compared to the magnitude of our possibilities. Thank you for proving that one person's commitment to helping others can literally reshape the world.

Rest in peace, knowing that your life's work was not in vain. Rest in peace, knowing that your voice continues to echo in the hearts and minds of those you've touched. Rest in peace, knowing that the seeds you planted are still growing, still bearing fruit, still transforming lives in ways you may never have imagined.

Your physical presence may have departed this realm, but your influence remains powerfully alive in every success story you helped create, in every dream you helped nurture, in every life you helped transform from ordinary to extraordinary.

I'll continue to listen to your teachings for many years to come, finding fresh insights and renewed inspiration with each encounter. Your wisdom has become a permanent part of my internal guidance system, a compass that will continue pointing me toward growth, contribution, and fulfilment.

The student in me will forever be grateful to the teacher you were. The success I've achieved will forever be connected to the foundation you helped me build. The life I'm living will forever bear the imprint of the principles you so generously shared.

Thank you, Sir, for everything you gave to this world. Thank you for making it possible for someone like me to discover what was truly possible. Thank you for the privilege of being touched by your wisdom and transformed by your teachings.

Until we meet again in whatever realm awaits us beyond this physical existence, I carry your lessons forward with deep appreciation and unwavering commitment to honour the gift you gave me by using it to help others find their own path to transformation.

Vale, Bob Proctor. Your work here is complete, but your legacy lives on in every life you touched, every dream you helped birth, and every impossible thing you taught us was actually inevitable.

Farewell, mentor. Farewell, teacher. Farewell, friend.

The torch you lit burns brightly still.

ABOUT THE AUTHOR

Adrian Maxwell's life story reads like a testament to the transformative power of persistence, self-belief, and the willingness to embrace second chances. Born and raised in a low socio-economic working-class suburb of Australia, Adrian's early years were shaped by the modest circumstances and practical challenges that define life in communities where dreams often seem like luxuries few can afford.

Despite these humble beginnings, Adrian possessed an imagination that soared far beyond the boundaries of his immediate environment. He dreamed of an exciting future filled with creativity, purpose, and meaningful contribution to the world around him. These weren't idle fantasies but genuine aspirations that burned brightly within him, even during his darkest moments.

However, Adrian's adolescence proved to be a particularly challenging period that tested his resilience in ways no young person should have to endure. His teenage years were marred by significant family issues that created instability and emotional turmoil at home, precisely when he needed support and guidance most. Simultaneously, he faced persistent bullying problems at school that made his educational environment feel more like a battlefield than a place of learning and growth.

These twin pressures, domestic struggles and academic persecution, created a perfect storm that derailed Adrian's early educational journey. Like many young people overwhelmed by circumstances beyond their control, he initially failed at school, his academic potential suffocated by the weight of his personal challenges and the system's inability to recognise the extraordinary person struggling beneath the surface difficulties.

Yet Adrian's story is far from one of permanent defeat. In a remarkable demonstration of human resilience and the power of second chances, he made the courageous decision to return to education as an adult learner. This wasn't simply about completing unfinished business, it was about reclaiming his future and proving to himself that his early setbacks didn't define his ultimate potential.

With newfound maturity, purpose, and determination, Adrian embarked on an extraordinary academic journey that would see him not just complete his basic education, but excel far beyond what anyone, including himself, might have originally imagined possible. He pursued his studies with the passion of someone who truly understood the value of education, eventually achieving success at master's degree level.

This academic transformation opened the door to a career that perfectly married his intellectual capabilities with his desire to make a positive difference in others' lives. Adrian became an English teacher, a profession that allowed him to share his love of language, literature, and learning with young people who may have been facing their own challenges and uncertainties.

But Adrian's creative ambitions extended beyond the classroom. Drawing upon his life experiences, his academic knowledge, and the wisdom gained through his journey of personal transformation, he transitioned into becoming an author. Through his writing, he has been able to reach an even broader audience, sharing insights and inspiration that stem directly from his own remarkable journey from despair to triumph.

Today, Adrian lives the life he once only dared to dream about during those difficult early years. He is happily married to a loving partner who shares his values and supports his continued growth and creative endeavours. Together, they are raising two children, providing them with the stable, nurturing environment that Adrian himself longed for during his own childhood.

Adrian's story serves as powerful proof that our beginnings need not determine our endings, that setbacks can become setups for remarkable comebacks, and that with the right mindset, persistent effort, and perhaps the guidance of wise mentors like Bob Proctor, it's possible to transform even the most challenging circumstances into the foundation for an extraordinary life.

His journey from a struggling teenager in working-class Australia to a successful educator, author, and family man demonstrates that no matter how dark the starting point, there is always a pathway to the light, if we have the courage to seek it and the persistence to follow it, regardless of how long or difficult that journey might prove to be.

www.ingramcontent.com/pod-product-compliance
Lightning Source LLC
Chambersburg PA
CBHW060002300526
45794CB00003B/1045